Unfolding the Field

Unfolding the Field

Left Fork

O'Brien, Oregon

Michael
Spring

Josephine Community Libraries
Grants Pass, Oregon

Also by Michael Spring

Books
Blue Crow
Mudsong
Root of Lightning

Chapbooks
Dancing on Earth
Acoustic Trees
Light and Shadows
Moving Through Stone
Gutter Therapy
Edge of Blue
Blue Wolf
Ravenwood

Copyright © 2016 Michael Spring
ISBN-13 978-1-945824-00-5
First Left Fork Edition
July 2016

for Treesong

contents

1

2

3

4

5

Unfolding the Field

The moon drops one or two feathers into the field.
The dark wheat listens.

James Wright

walking away

the neighborhood dogs didn't hear me
when I climbed over the fence
and passed the yellow plastic Buddha
and the smashed grocery cart tangled in ivy

I walked around the brambles
and the hobo camps
where hotdogs burned on garbage can lids

when I found the red clay banks
I followed the river
looking for rainbows on the surface of fish

I walked under the tree
where Regino hanged himself
beyond the brown scum of river shallows
and the muck gripping tin cans
and broken bottles

I walked over mildewed clothes
to avoid stepping on the dead gull

I'm lucky the neighborhood dogs didn't hear me
as I followed the river
over boulders and fallen trees
into a field of tall grass

threads

what I'm looking for is a pair of scissors
to cut an opening in the fabric between this world
and the world where you've disappeared

what I want is another chthonic conversation
in the underground fort of our youth
and the owl feather you gave me to place above my bed

you said this feather will give me the gift of vision
I want to see the pattern the threads will make
and the landscape the pattern will resemble

what I want is a field I can unfold before my feet
and the full moon tethered to the path before me
I'm looking for a place to let loose my shadow

the circus train

here's another field
harboring the railroad track

stitched like a scar
between the city and the desert

*

tonight we'll vanish again
and the field will turn back

into coyote and jack rabbit
flashing in the headlights
of dusty cars

*

the clacking sound of the train
is inside of me

I can hear it in the cicadas
in the juniper
and in the tumbleweed

*

home is an invisible rope
stretched tight

from one field to another

jazz in the time of war

it's here once again
the news of a loved one
deployed overseas

our eyes search the room
for something to grasp onto

we open the window
and find a planet floating
over stars

we declare everything's OK
as we turn off the TV
and tune into jazz

Bill Evans is on piano
bleeding blue sounds into green

we want the music to soothe us
but tonight it moves our thoughts
into a fog we cannot see through

fractured glass

annexes of color
stab:

Picasso-like blades –

a mask
for my reflection

*

I want biopic
visions

answers tethered
and pensive

*

I discover another
notebook page

*I'm not there
was I ever there?*

*

my heart sits in a bowl
in a daydream

what cuts me
is the sky I love:

dusk through a glass
of merlot –

the blood I want
for my hands

portal

after Vivian Fine's "Portal: for Violin and Piano"

when I found her piano in the forest
I leaned over the lid warily
as if looking into a bog –

the shadows below the trees were green
and black – heavy
as a bridge

the trees creaked in the wind as I began
performing *Portal*

the dark wood of the piano
was polished slick as glass

my image swam to the surface

reclamation

I reclaim the stitches
the doctor pulled from my chest
and the blood and the blue light
that flooded my dreams

I reclaim the oxygen tent
and the fluids that pumped
through the machines
and the hole in my heart
the surgery repaired

I reclaim the news of the lunar missions
and my first glass of Tang

I reclaim my bedroom window
that portal I climbed through
to meet friends in the park

I reclaim the sweet smell of roots
and the upturned earth
and my underground fort
where I often entered
to be alone with the world

I reclaim the mushrooms I ate
which boiled the clouds
into bulbous knots and labyrinths
revealing music trapped inside

and finally I reclaim the Ouija board
I kept in my bookcase
the one that brought news from the dead
and sent my own ghost into orbit

Kafka on the wall

I do not know
who hung this painting here

the painting of a man's thin face
full of muscular shadows

I hear the lake in the walls
sluggish waves
and the shifting gravel

I will not sleep for fear
of someone in the woods

the moon is gibbous
pulling away from the trees

rattlesnake

there's the rattlesnake again
this time in my waking dream

yesterday a dead branch
latching onto my foot

today, submerged in dry leaves,
the eroding bungee cord

I've been holding on
to the coiling image, the actual
rattlesnake I saw last year, carefully
in a glass aquarium I formed in my mind

I'm tired of timidly studying
its movements and reactions

I smash the glass
allow the snake to pour forth

and follow the stream of muscle –

the flexible scales
feathering light

leaving Hell's Canyon

when we closed the root cellar door
we knew we wouldn't be back

we left the yams, beets, and greens
obscured in the dark

an assortment of fruits
and pickled vegetables
visceral in glass jars

you said the sod roof
would eventually break through
and the root cellar will rot
hidden in thickets of chaparral

a perfect den for rabbit or snake

when we walked away
the scent of sage and juniper
sweetened the air

and the dust
no matter how lightly we stepped
rose like smoke from the path

The world is full of magic things,
patiently waiting for our senses to grow sharper.

W. B. Yeats

djembe

I open my hands

for the goat skin stretched taut
over the goblet shaped hollow
of the hand-carved wood

I'm striking the drum, entering

the *duun guun* of the bass
the *pa ta* of the slap
the *go do* of the tone

shamans claim to fly
with such sounds, riding them
like horses over new plains

the drum is a vessel

I place my childhood inside
along with my dreams
and notions and fears

everything I am enters the drum

I close my eyes and witness
black and white images
finding color

I open my hands

rattlesnake speaks

because you summoned me
you want a psychological
venom – to become something *other* –
transmutable

and that is why I struck

now, slaked light from the imaginal
slides over your permeable synapsis, punctures
your outstretched perception

look: the madrone and tanoak
are dying in each other's arms –
mating or merging –

sinuously worshipping the essential struggle

even when the venom no longer
drums with your blood

and vision that surged and simmered
has sunk back into its malleable field

you will find yourself stronger
moving like water
past Port-Orford cedars and Western Azeala
over the ancient Takelma pathways

your thoughts will submerge
into the scaly slick flow of mudstone
and serpentine rock

and I will still be with you, a form of music
unwinding –

you will feel the warmth in your abdomen
as I pour upward – undulating –

a ghost through your heart and lungs –

my head inside your head – my eyes
languid behind your eyes –

mesmerized, you will slide
out of your old life
into the mellifluous waves of sunlight

colors of the sky

my two sisters climbed a tree
outside the hospital window
to sneak into my room after visiting hours

they saw my pulse caught in a machine
and translucent vines growing from my arm
into a bag hung from a hook

*

I remember the sunset that night
the colors in the sky
were the same colors as their dresses:

purple, azure, blushing red, ghost gray
and floating white

*

my chest was pried open like a wooden crate

and the doctor who breached my heart
stitched the murmuring hole closed

*

I was told the doctor saved my life

but it was my sisters
who filled me with the colors of the sky

1968

when I was five
I climbed the winding steps
of blue light

into that room behind the clock
the surgeons watched

and there was my body –

a child supine
on the operating table

*

my heart sat in its cavern
exposed to light

*

before I was buried
in the haze of anesthesia

I imagined the doctor
lifting my heart
and working it

like some sort of pull-apart
puzzle

*

I remember my parents
promised starfish
white sands and the surf

they handed me a wentletrap shell

as large as my heart

*

I looked through
the backside
of the surgery room's clock
and through the walls

to the steps of blue light

*

the clock before me
had no springs
or sprockets

but rather it was made
of sea shells

I reached in and pulled out
the wentletrap shell

*

I clutched the shell
and held it to my ear –

it was suddenly everything
I wanted –

absorbed in the sound
of the ocean

pelicans

the pelicans hover like claws
above the surf

I watch them drop
then disappear
into the ocean

I imagine kelp groves
with sea creatures
trolling below the surface

always I'm trying to enter
the dark light of mystery

I'm like my grandfather
the family crabber
sinking his one and only trap
from the wooden edge
of introspection

the pelicans emerge
filled with fish

a numinous pageant

visceral with a sky
pregnant
with more skies

vessels

much like a mushroom
after a storm
my ceramic cup
glimmers on the ground

still warm with coffee
I pick it up and pour
a dissolving depression
into the damp sand

the ocean stirs
below a leaden sky
memories move
in the surfeit foam

*

I see each of my children
the death of my friend
and my first blossom
from the erotic tree

and there are my longings
and brushes with death

as my pulse is pulled
into thrashing waves

*

the wind is full of salt and sting
I squint my eyes
watching a crab boat crawl
over the choppy ocean

I'm slaked on this beach
having declined
to board that boat
now disappearing in fog

the mask

when I pulled the mask from the wall
water poured into the room

that is why I no longer wear the mask

I will not risk flooding my home

I no longer care if I am
a better neighbor or friend
when it's on

I will glue the mask onto the wall
it is now a lock – a guardian –
no longer my face

fishing with my son

we're golfing with fishing poles:
from one picnic bench to the other
we cast lures and sinkers
over the glassy park grass

the sky is overcast with occasional
late morning joggers and jogger-nots

and with little surprise we see
a scuffed up soccer ball
in the tall grass

after several sightings all morning
from The Interzone Café rooftop
to the sloughs near the mint field
we're sure this soccer ball followed us
bouncing off bumpers
and windshields as we drove the highway

it is the head from our now headless scarecrow
we thought lost
after punting it into the field

it's eyeballing us for the opportunity to trip us
(and it is tripping us out)

I admit I'm fond of this soccer ball
as it appears when we're not sure
what to say to each other

even though you're my son
we're still getting to know each other

the senseless helps us make sense
of each other

OK, I'll shut up, *soccer ball head*
must be exhausted as it has stopped moving
near the last picnic bench in our course

if we can plunk the head with a sinker
we'll be able to capture it

then when it wakes
it'll be with its body again
stuffed with last year's crumpled news

are you ready?
let's concentrate
and make that one pure cast

to a child in the wilderness

look at you on the wooden platform

a conductor
with a willow switch

the lake before you must be
a body of music

once, long ago, I too stood
upon this platform, flying

with imagination's feathered serpent

and entered
the world the world was offering

the scent of fennel still saunters
influencing perception

what am I now seeing?
the muscular inflections
of your symphony?

I witness an emerald green wake –

a blessing – that water-like flame
from the manzanita's hummingbird

but before you see me
I drift backward through brush

I do not want you to mute any sounds
you've opened

it is important you can explore
in solitude, unhindered

I find an old deer path
and follow it deeper into the forest

I, too, am blessed – unfettered –
after all these years –

even as the shadows of trees
are encroaching with heavy wings –

I'm now a strand of music

bear speaks

when you need me
I'll rush toward you
the way a mountain would
all grace in tumble, rumbling
like a newly formed planet
my head made up
of a thousand other heads
my eyes filled
with the light of a star (a star made up
of a thousand other stars)

my body will surge forward
all earth-tones roiling towards black
and void
and fringed with sylvan light

I'll leap from constellation into you

I'll take you into the heart
of the mountain

3

If you surrendered to the air, you could ride it.

Toni Morrison

new tribe

a mosh pit of trees
has caught the moon

no wonder a group of teens
stomp and howl
around the bonfire

and drummers stir
the dark forest
into a frenetic dance

*

the cross-dressing shaman
sloughs off his blue slip
and purple brassiere –

an offering he says –
and tosses them into the fire

an ancestor always appears
after Peter Sears

the first time I fell in love
it was the Choctaw bone-picker
who appeared –

the grandfather of the grandmother
of my father –

revered by the tribe for singing
to spirits
and plucking flesh from bones –

long fingernails
akin to the vulture's talons

he'd burn and scrape the bones
until they were slivers of moon

then bundled them like sacred scrolls
to place in a mound of earth

the girl I was with confessed
she too communicated with spirits

maybe that's why we kissed –
but it was the bone-picker who took over
with an assertiveness
I claim alien to my temperament

he pressed as close
as a ghost can get to flesh

the girl leaned toward me
but maybe it wasn't her

maybe it was her ancestor
craving the touch of mine

siblings of Dogtown

driven by stories of Dogtown
we abandoned our speed bump jumps

to scuff our skateboards
in the concrete bowl
of an emptied pool

I remember sitting on the edge
with friends, drumming boards
with our fingers, anxious

to crouch low and surf
the curved concrete

as if in the pipeline
of a *bitchin* white-cap crashing

we all wanted to be the one
who nailed the first tail-tapped trick
and aerial

spinning sunlight
into polyurethane wheels

*

we were the children of stardust
tossed from a zephyr

*

we were also siblings
of the dark blonde, the veteran
of shock therapy, spinning

and flashing a butterfly knife
on the street corner

*

as craft entered our angst
we knew we could hawk the air

finding freedom in a flipped board, grabbed
in mid-flight

family time monopoly

I wasn't interested in winning as much
as I wanted to be *the man on horseback*
riding around the world

for me, the best part of the game
was choosing my token

if my sister-in-law, the family champion, selected
the man on horseback then I'd choose *the dog*

and then my only chance at fun
would be to piss on her Park Place doorstep
before scampering off the board

digging for words

I used the spade to dig their roots
but the spade is no longer
available for digging

it has been captured
by some thick rooted words
and is now kept hidden in the tunnels
inside my brain

*

I have come to understand the spade
has been fashioned into a weapon
for my own protection

and has been made accessible
only to a select group of words:
well dressed words
wearing dark shades

*

I can only imagine how the spade
has been changed: pounded
down in a fire, forged into a sword

or stretched long into a proboscis
or scorpion tail

*

even in my thoughts as I form words –
as I glance at myself in the mirror
spiteful at my predicament –

I can feel the fragments of the spade
fractioning and reforming
into throwing stars

goat rock

I stood as a rocky ledge
overlooking
the canyon

leaning into the drift
of fog

*

a goat beside me
lifted its head
as if to bleat

but it wasn't
a goat

it was an outcrop
of rock –

an argument
against contentment

the neighbor's garbage

the ravens have strewn
the neighbor's garbage
across the dirt road

soggy bags and rotting
vegetables mixed with wads
of duct tape and broken glass

buried in a heap of flour
is a plastic dildo
under an egg carton

the underwear I lift
with a stick hangs heavy
with syrup and rose petals

I know this is random material –
household flotsam –
but I now see my neighbors
in strange scenarios

I should clean up this mess
but instead I fling the underwear
onto a low branch

the ravens in the leaves
above my head
chatter and cheer

the underwear
looks like a melted face

let the next person
passing by
stumble here
let them wonder

let them try
to make sense of this

origins

*In a cave in the Indonesian island of Sulawesi 14 prehistoric paintings
including 12 human hand stencils, two naturalistic animal depictions –
one showing an animal called a babirusa or "pig-deer", and the other
showing a pig – date back to at least 40,000 years ago could be the oldest
known figurative work of art in the world.*
        study published in Nature, *2014*

pig and pig-deer
these are the images we found
in the Indonesian cave

not the wild, wild horses
and not the saber-toothed cave lions

and not Sasquatch
or bubble-headed astronauts

it's the pig that accompanies
the prehistoric stains
of human hands

and what if we could crawl deeper
into the image?
perhaps we'd find
what the pig digested
or what is behind it
hidden from view

perhaps we'd discover
the *I am nature* source
that lit up the walls
inside Jackson Pollack's head –

a drooling landscape
an explosion –
the dribble and splatter
of a cosmic nature

ghazal for music

my sister is at her desk reading a score sheet of music
she's going to dedicate her life to the theory of music

this time it's Mozart who opens the door for me
I didn't expect to walk into the world of music

yesterday a man entered the square with a gourd
he claims it saved his life – it was filled with music

I'm not sure how to approach my grandmother on her deathbed
she's talking to the TV – *it's lost all sense of music*

look at you now, Mr. Spring, climbing to the top of that tree
yes, we've heard your banter about trees making music

ghazal with foraging goats

the goats move like a controlled burn, foraging
        below the rocky ledges of a mountain
I look at storm clouds sublimating shadows
        between us and the distant Lone Mountain

last night I dreamed of a saber-toothed tiger
        with fur as reflective as water
I believe the ancient cat was an embodiment
        of all that is wild inside the mountain

your fingers touched the reflection of your fingers
        as you stirred the water in the pond
koi fish swam into the reflection of your body as your body
        stood in the reflection of a mountain

the goats found their way to the garden as we yelled
        and clapped and stamped our feet
but they wouldn't budge and continued browsing
        glancing up with the sagacity of mountains

the trail I chose brought me to a dead end unless I dare
        to wade through a bog of cobra lilies
I won't pretend I know where I'm going – although
        I'm not lost – I can see Lone Mountain

ghazal for the cave

our dreams are structured like a cave?
how many chambers are in this cave?

a salamander muses in a stream
lulling in the limestone of the cave

guano muck and slip of vaporous glisten
stag of a stalactite drools in the cave

I didn't find the cave, it found me
I crave the water trickle muse of a cave

is anybody there? who's here?
no, I won't drown in the collective fear of caves

I stop to face the darkness in me
wolfed by the darkness of a cave

wet mouth of a mountain surrounds me
seducing me with the moonmilk of a cave

mother of mycelium and root of dreaming
will you embrace me in this cave?

in this wet and dripping grotto
extinguish the lamp and become the cave

bridge menu

I'll say no to the house special – *the Emperor's Green Spine* adorned with jade

and I'm not interested in *the Metallic Truss with Wind Chime Cables*

I don't want to simply cross a river
to another city or tourist trap

I've decided on the *Amazonian Cliff to Cliff*
although it might upset my stomach

I like the simplicity of bamboo and rope
leading into the trees full of birds

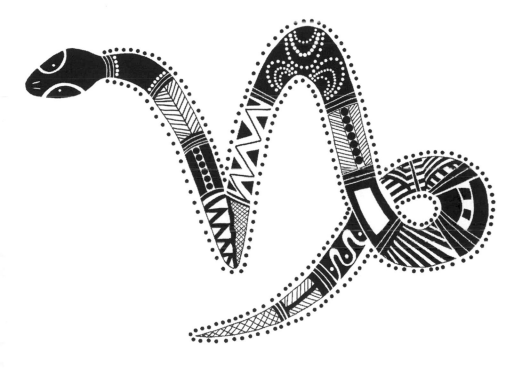

4

Our truest life is when we are in dreams awake.

Henry David Thoreau

crossing the river at flood stage

crossing the century-old truss bridge
I still see the tower from last night's dream

what caused the tower to sink into the stony ground?
the sky's golden haze conveys the notion
that the tower will rise, fully amplified, once
I step off the other end

it is also a matter of stepping past procrastination

how many times did I say I'd come back
to this field where
in my youth
I'd walk to disappear?

*

to enter this tower is to become the field
of tall grass with its four-chambered cave
sequestered under the granite boulder

*

today is dangerous, but rare

I ignore the orange cones and the yellow
"do not cross" tape

the wooden planks of the bridge want to tear free
and tumble

water surges, rattling the old
bolts in the metal

caught in the truss frame web
the bridge seduces me with a sway
like the throb of a lake
with its lone fisherman in a boat

*

I'm absorbed in the sound of the river

that resounds
in the wind-thrashed trees

*

imagine being swallowed
into a world that reveals black
as a color of all colors

if you gaze long enough you'll see
the rousing iridescence
similar to the oracular portals in the peacock's plume

*

what of the tower?
dreams slide like mercury from burning cinnabar –

the tower unravels
from bedrock: becomes the field

*

to cross this bridge is to become the tower

*

as the embankments of the river – including the town

with its outdoor theatre
and its one café –

including the hospital on the hill
where I was born –

now dissolve

my former self sheds with each step forward

5

We can wake up in a place where everything hangs off the edges,
creating itself.

Brenda Hillman

raven speaks

if I get the chance I'll split your eye in two
my beak will snap and clack after each fleeting half

your eye will become two then four then eight
your other eye will float above, witnessing
a storm of shadow, a whirlwind of light

if I get the chance I'll crack open your head
for you to capture the subtle pitches
and timbres from trees

along with the thrumming of the earthworm
and the drumming of the sphinx moth

you need me often in your life, but not always
when you want me

many times, like now, I'll be ravenous
to cut something from you

you might say my feathers are blackened from creation
or burnt after stealing the sun
I won't deny this – I'm multiple
just as my colors are compressed
into what you perceive as black

you will see only what you can see
but that is why I'm here:
creating bones for clouds, caves from stars

with black mirrors for eyes

road trip (after pulling the Death card from the Tarot deck)

the wheat field
on fire
with sunlight

makes me stop my car
in the middle
of the road

*

no longer running
with the bombast
of punk jazz
I open the door
and leave

the city's image
on the dirty windshield

*

I ditch my plans
as I'm now listening
to the field
thrumming
in the brushed tones
of light

*

green and purple rocks
boil
to the surface:

a distant mountain
and its forest
fuse with dusk

*

Idiot! a man shouts
from a moving car
*get your junk
out of the road!*

he punches his horn
and stomps the gas

*

I continue wading
further
into the field

my body
devouring sunlight

blue wolf

the howl rises from the forest
turning the black night blue

*

I shift my weight
from heel to toe
persistent and slow

as if wading
through a field full of deer

*

if my breast bone were cracked
and pried open I swear
something other than my heart
and lungs
would pour out –

perhaps a blue wolf would escape
and disappear
into the black ridge
heavy with trees

*

I tilt my head, listening
with the concentration of stitching
a wound closed

junco

for over a month its brassy-yellow beak
battles my window

hooded like a bandit, it stabs
staccato, with laconic heartbeats –
a complicated philosophy

Pueblos called it the snow bird
that drags rain and snow
like a blanket trailing behind a sleepy child

but this junco is not sleepy
it's fixated on cracking open the beak
of its double

my neighbor said it must be a male thing
one attacked the side mirrors
of her Chevy truck all spring

I drink my coffee and tap the keypad
as the junco taps the window –
how long will this last?
will it damage its brain? will it
damage mine?

I wonder if I'll soon find
the poor bird knocked out
or dead

last week, in April, snow fell
for the first time in over a year

my lover says the snow bird has something to say
that I must capture its message
before it will leave

but I can't imagine it gone –
every morning it drums
as I reflect

snow bird, stay as long as you can!

wind storm

it never occurred to me until this storm-day, while swinging in the wind, that trees are travelers.

John Muir

no longer nestled in the understory
of groaning branches
I brave the storm

lashed by wind
I clutch the pinnacle
of the pine tree

I won't turn away
if life flashes before me

I don't have a death wish
I'm simply traveling
with the trees

thrashing into the numinous
swaying back and forth
and back again

the hearth

whether it is a Rumford or a pit
or a mass of brick

it is the fire
that draws us close

our hands opening
for the heat

*

the logs in the flames
look like limbs
torn from a torso
or bones:

the sacrum or columns
of a spine

or a crumbling skull

*

perhaps the skull is in
the position of bowing
to the earth

where it melts and becomes
a surface for shifting images

*

I'll throw more wood
into the hearth

forget about the movie
tonight

nothing replaces fire

round window

after a day of chopping wood
pitching manure
and stacking stones
we stand outside

looking at our kitchen's round window
as if it were the light
of a second moon

the skin of our earthen house
holds the window

perhaps the window is more mouth than eye
pulling us inside
where we will fire up the wood stove

and listen to the tea kettle quake
below the peeled poles holding the loft
where we sleep

the river is wider

after thirty years the old farmhouse
is a few degrees off from where
my memory said it would be

and the river is wider
and the red clay banks
are brown with a hint of blue

the quarry I now scurry about
used to be a green pond
full of frogs and crawdads

I walk past the cement bike bridge
that replaced the rickety footbridge

there's the smoky smell of fennel
and the brassy mint
mixing with the new park's odor
of freshly cut grass

the children skipping rocks in the shallows
look familiar – perhaps they are
children of the friends I once knew

how will the repeating dreams I have
of this place now translate in my brain?

the clay banks of my subconscious

must be turning soft and malleable
reforming into something else

after thirty years I find
the rope swing tree
from which I used to launch myself
over the water

and the golden leaves
that just now float back into memory
look like fish flashing in the wind

acknowledgments

Grateful acknowledgments to the following publications where these poems first appeared (sometimes in different versions):

Absinthe Poetry Review (fractured glass, raven speaks, rattlesnake speaks, threads, to a child in the wilderness)
Allegro Poetry Magazine (djembe, pelicans)
Atticus Review (blue wolf)
Blue Lyra Review (bear speaks, ghazal for music)
Chiron Review (road trip)
Cirque (Kafka on the wall, neighbor's garbage, reclamation, the river is wider)
Flowstone (portal)
Flyway; Journal of Writing and Environment (round window)
Galway Review (the mask)
Gargoyle (jazz in the time of war, new tribe)
Hermes Poetry Journal (the hearth, fishing with my son, ghazal for the cave, origins)
Innisfree Poetry Journal (leaving Hell's Canyon)
Modern Poetry Quarterly Review (crossing the river at flood stage)
Neon Literary Magazine (circus train, 1968)
Poetry Pacific (vessels)
Sleet (colors of the sky)
Spillway (digging for words)
Toe Good Poetry (an ancestor always appears, bridge menu, family time monopoly, siblings of Dogtown,)
Turtle Island Quarterly (ghazal with foraging goats, junco, rattlesnake, walking away, windstorm)

Some of these poems have been reprinted in the following
publications: *Lummox*, poetrymagazine.com, *Steelhead Special*,
The 2016 Rhysling Anthology, *Takilma Common Ground*.

Several of these poems appeared in the chapbook *Blue Wolf*,
winner of The 2013 Turtle Island Poetry Award, awarded by
Turtle Island Quarterly.

Thanks to Sara Backer, Wyn Cooper, and Carter McKenzie for
their valuable input with these poems.

dedications

"bear speaks" is for Eaden and Silver Bear

"colors of the sky" is for my sisters Cindy and Cheryl

"fishing with my son" is for Max

"ghazal for the cave" is for
The Oregon Caves National Monument

"ghazal with foraging goats" is for Treesong

"jazz in the time of war" is for Justin and Stephanie Bahler

"junco," "the hearth," and "round window"
are for Hazel Danene

"leaving Hell's Canyon" is for Pamela Steele

The rattlesnake poems are for Dan Speer, Eko, and Treesong

"threads" is for Erick Johnson

"walking away" is for Chris Fujita

"wind storm" is for Paulann Petersen

about the art

Grateful acknowledgement to the following artists for the use of their images:

Deborah Ann Dawson - "Talking Crows" (cover and title page painting). Visit deborahanndawson.com to see more.

Justine Glass (IkaikaDesign) - *Circle of Life* (page 3), *Earth's Spirit* (page 21), *Barsoom Royal Ink* (page 38), *Ursa Chief* (page 43), *Aboriginal Capricorn* (page 67), and *Raven Guardian* (page 75).

Simon Hojer - *Tribal 3* (page 60)

Kiko Picasso - *Tribal Wolf with musical theme* (page 82)

about the author

Michael Spring is the author of three previous books. His first book, *Blue Crow*, was translated into Portuguese by the University of the Azores. A selection from his second book, *Mudsong*, won the 2004 Robert Graves Award. In 2007 Oregon State University Library and Poetry Northwest named *Mudsong* one of 150 outstanding poetry books in Oregon's 150-year history. His third book, *Root of Lightning*, was awarded an honorable mention for the 2012 Eric Hoffer Book Award. A recent chapbook, *Blue Wolf*, won the 2013 Turtle Island Poetry Award.

Michael recently won a 2016 Luso-American Fellowship from DISQUIET International, and is featured reading a poem in collaboration with composer-musician Martin Birke on the CD *Your Sleekest Engine* by Genre Peak (Gonzo Multimedia, 2016). He lives in southern Oregon.

63068052R00061

Made in the USA
Charleston, SC
26 October 2016